SCAM PROOF YOUR LIFE IN THE END TIMES

Justice & Restoration for Christians

STEVE CIOCCOLANTI

DISCOVER
MEDIA

MEET STEVE CIOCCOLANTI

Steve Cioccolanti, B.A., M.Ed., is a five-time #1 Best-selling author on Amazon. With over 52 million views, he is one of the most watched Christian YouTubers worldwide.

Watch and subscribe here:
www.YouTube.com/DiscoverMinistries

Born in Thailand to a family of Buddhists, Catholics, Methodists, and Muslims, Cioccolanti has a unique perspective and practical insights into spiritual life. He leads an international church and ministry in Melbourne, Australia.

Having travelled to more than 45 nations, Cioccolanti is a sought after speaker on hot topics such as end-time prophecy, Biblical justice, world religions and breaking news from a Christian perspective. He is currently authoring more books, filming more videos, and sharing Biblical truths around the world.

Join Online Church!
www.DiscoverChurch.online

Partner with Discover Ministries
www.Discover.org.au/Give

Partner with USA Church
(Tax-deductible giving for US residents only)
www.USAChurch.Online

To book Pastor Steve Cioccolanti for your church or event, contact: info@discover.org.au

Connect with Steve Cioccolanti on social media:

- facebook.com/discoverministry
- twitter.com/cioccolanti
- patreon.com/cioccolanti
- amazon.com/author/newyorktimesbestseller

Scam Proof Your Life in the End Times: *Justice & Restoration for Christians*

Published by Discover Media www.discover.org.au

© 2021 Steve Cioccolanti www.discoverchurch.online

Unless otherwise noted, all Scripture quotations are taken from New King James Version of the Bible. Copyright © 1979, 1980, 1982. Used by permission of Thomas Nelson, Inc., Publishers.

Scriptures taken from other versions are marked as below:

(ESV) The ESV® Bible (The Holy Bible, English Standard Version®) © 2001 by Crossway Bibles, a publishing ministry of Good News Publishers. Used by permission.

(GNT) the Good News Translation in Today's English Version - Second Edition © 1992 by American Bible Society. Used by Permission.

(NET) are from the New English Translation.

(NIV) are from the New International Version. © 1973, 1978, 1984. Used by permission of International Bible Society.

(NLT) are from the New Living Translation © 1996. Used by permission of Tyndale House Publishers.

Cover design by *Esther Jun & Selena Sok*

Paperback ISBN   978-1-922273-44-4

Ebook ISBN 978-1-922273-45-1

Printed in U.S.A.

CONTENTS

INTRODUCTION

THE PROBLEM THAT YOU SEE IS THE PROBLEM THAT YOU'RE CALLED TO SOLVE.

A lot of people don't realize that. They see a problem, and rather than solving it, what do they do? They complain about it.

In reality, you may notice a problem that others don't because it's your **distinctive gift to solve it**. For instance, you hear an instrument out of tune. Well, not everybody hears that. An amateur may not hear it, or he may hear it but not be bothered by it. But an expert musician cannot tolerate it. The more musically gifted you are, the more demanding you will be that an instrument be perfectly tuned.

So if you're sitting in a church and hear somebody singing out of tune, rather than saying, "Well, he's a bad musician," it's possible your calling is to join the worship team. You see, rather than complaining about your church, join the worship team and make it better. You could offer voice coaching, singing lessons, piano tutoring, or some other musical contribution. The problem you see is a clue to the problem you've been put on earth to solve. In my case, I've always noticed one thing. Ever since I was little, I can't escape it.

I always notice INJUSTICE.

It bugs me. I realize that not everyone is bugged, but it peeves me, it angers me, and it motivates me. I don't like injustice for anybody. In fact, I'm not as bothered when it's done to me because my faith is in God to restore me. I'm more bothered by injustice to others because they may not know what to do. I don't like to see people get deceived or abused.

I think about it.

I think about injustice during the day. Sometimes it just pops into my head. Sometimes an injustice is far removed from me, but it will pop into my head or into my heart, and I'll start thinking about it.

I think about it at night. I think about it during the day. And I think about how to solve it.

When I became a Christian at the age of 20, I didn't see the Bible as the solution to injustice at first, mainly because I was a baby Christian. I saw God as the solution for my personal sins. God had to work on me first before I could help others. God had to clean me up from my addictions and personal flaws. However, when I learned and understood the love of God, the goodness of God, and the right-standing (righteousness) of the believer through

Jesus Christ, I could go on to study other topics that were important to God and not just to me.

The Lord soon led me into Bible prophecy, and my ministry exploded on social media. Viewership magnified when I taught publicly on the end time. The end time is often misrepresented as a message of doom and gloom, because "end time" sounds like "end of the world." No, contrary to what you might have been told or believe, the world is not going to end. The Earth was created to last forever. *"Generations come and generations go, but the earth remains forever,"* (Ecclesiastes 1:4 NIV). God compares His eternal sanctuary in Heaven to the Earth. Heaven is *"Like the earth which He has established forever"* (Psalm 78:69). Rather than being destroyed, the Earth will actually be cleansed and renewed at Jesus' Coming.

Yes, there will be momentary tribulation for Jews and persecution of Christians, but the main message of the end times is not about us. It's about Jesus coming back to right the wrongs, to restore what was lost, to reward the believers, and to punish the evildoers. This is all Good News if you have become Christian and are not among those being judged by Christ!

My study of the end times naturally opened my eyes to God's end-time goal—in a word, it's *justice.*

One of the key Scriptures the Lord led me to was this.

DEUTERONOMY 32:4
...For all His ways are justice,

I was very happy to see that in Deuteronomy 32:4, the

Bible says that, **"ALL God's ways are justice"** [emphasis added].

Say that to yourself, say it to God, say it to the devil, **"ALL His ways are justice."**

THE SECRET TO INTERPRETING THE BIBLE AND UNDERSTANDING END-TIME PROPHECY

I learned the secret to interpreting the Bible and understanding end-time theology (or eschatology): **"ALL His ways are justice."** All His ways are NOT mercy and grace; all His ways are NOT fulfilling your needs and your desires; ALL His ways are JUSTICE.

If you don't understand this about God, that His nature is just and everything that's going on in the world is to prove His justice, you won't understand the Bible and you won't understand Him.

A lot of people think, "Why doesn't God just prove Himself to me? Just show up! Just prove that He exists!" Isn't the answer obvious?

He doesn't want to. It's not His priority. He could care less about proving His existence to you. What He cares about is justice—**"For all His ways are justice."** Psalm 37:28 adds, "For the Lord LOVES justice..." [emphasis mine]. Everything that's being allowed on Earth is to prove His commitment to justice.

Now, you might question, "Well, then, why is the world all messed up?"

It is because one of the things that God wants to prove to all Creation for all eternity is that He is NOT an unjust dictator. If He intervened whenever He disagreed with us, if He did what He would like to do, which is to stop every sinner, then 100% of the planet would be dead. That's the truth—100%. There's no way to stop sinners from sinning except by ending every opportunity for them to sin, and that is only possible by ending their lives.

God could stop sin right now. Would He prove that He's powerful? Yes. Would He prove that He exists? Yes. And then what? He wouldn't have proven His justice. In fact, without His incredible restraint, all the people who die and go to hell would merely shake their fists at Him for all eternity and say, "You are an unjust God, You didn't even give me a chance." So God says, "Alright, I'll give you a chance." So every sinner who's allowed to live increases the suffering on the earth.

Sinners are not reasonable or easy to please. They claim they wish God would show up and intervene in this suffering world. But if He started with you and intervened by saying, "Hey! You're supposed to go to church," we already know the average sinner's response, "I don't want to." What if God (or His agent, a human messenger) were to insist, "You're supposed to go to church." That insistence would not meet with better results. The sinner would merely yell, "Get out of my face!"

If God were to show up through the wall or through the ceiling and remind you of all the things you are supposed to do, guess what? You'd hate Him. Maybe not you, my reader, since you have distinguished yourself to be the more open-minded of the species, but the general "you" out there in the world. Many people out there would shake their fists at God and say, "What an unjust God—Leave me alone!"

"Leave me alone" is what many teenagers say to their parents. And what do you, as parents, eventually realize? You have to leave them alone because they're going to have to learn the hard way.

My children usually believe me, but even if they don't, I know that they will eventually learn that in the big things of life, I was right because I'm older, I'm wiser, and I've already made all the same mistakes they're about to make.

However, many times your children are not going to believe your wisdom till they fall flat on their faces. The danger is that some people cannot recover from some mistakes. Some mistakes are fatal. Overdosing on drugs. Illicit sex with someone infected with HIV AIDS. Not managing your temper. Committing a crime. These are real dangers parents have to be concerned about.

So God is not so different from good earthly parents. He waits patiently for some of His Creation to come to the mature realization that He is wise even when they fail to fully understand His ways. All His ways are justice.

The above is merely one illustration—one facet of His justice. I'm merely introducing a new perspective to you, without going further into details. I'm suggesting that you will understand everything in the Bible, everything going on on Earth, and everything in the universe when you realize that ALL His ways are JUSTICE. But that's a broader subject for another book.

Suffice it to say, for the purpose of our conversation, when we become a truly transformed (or born again)

Christian, we join a divine family that is centered on justice. It's very strange to me to be a Christian and not be concerned about justice because it's God's number one thing.

It is a just thing that all humanity bows to Jesus because He is the only perfect human being who ever lived, and He came from Heaven to pay for our sins. After Jesus died and rose from the dead, He went to Heaven to allow everyone on earth a grace period to hear His Good News without force, coercion or heavy-handed tactics. He sent His witnesses to preach and commissioned them to write everything essential to our salvation in one book—the Bible. He continues to send preachers and pastors like myself out into the world to make known the choice sinners have: to turn from their sins, trust in Jesus' sacrifice and be saved.

However, Jesus will not wait forever for people to believe in Him because while He waits, more sin accumulates on the earth. With each passing day, sinners keep on sinning and people keep on suffering. So Jesus promised to come back and end the offer of salvation. The angels told the original disciples who watched Him ascend into Heaven, *"This same Jesus, who was taken up from you into heaven, will so come in like manner as you saw Him go into heaven"* (Acts 1:11b).

When Jesus returns, what will He do? *He's going to judge the living and the dead.* That's His first priority.

2 TIMOTHY 4:1 (NLT)
I solemnly urge you in the presence of God and

Christ Jesus, who will someday judge the living and the dead when he comes to set up his Kingdom:

There's no pit stop in between. There's no Santa Claus coming down the chimney to hand out a few gifts on the way. God the Father will send God the Son to earth a second time to prove HIS justice.

It's all about God proving that He was *just* to allow the Lord Jesus Christ to be sacrificed and crucified on the Cross to pay for our sins. The price of sin is death and there was no other way to rescue us but for the only perfect Man who ever lived to suffer on our behalf.

We should say, "Thank You Lord Jesus that You did all that for me!" It is a just and rightful thing that all men, women and children everywhere bow their knees to Jesus and confess He is their Lord. But many people are unjust— they won't do the right thing.

For those of us who've chosen to repent of our sins and accept Jesus' gift of salvation, not only have we been invited into this family, but we've also been given the authority to do something on earth about injustice. And I don't think we use our authority enough.

So today I want to talk to you about one small area where we can learn how to use our authority. I want to talk to you about something that many of you, my dear readers, have experienced.

If you're an honest person, you will be surprised by *scams*.

If you are not in the habit of lying, if you're not a

scammer, you will be very surprised by how many scammers are out there in the world. Some are big scammers. Some are small scammers. Some of you have been scammed as a child. Some of you have been scammed as an adult.

I WAS SCAMMED

I remember when I lived in southern France, around the age of 15 to 16, one of the Muslim boys that was in my Year 10 (French *troisieme*) said to me, "I'll pick you up for a concert" by this particular band that we all liked.

My host family told me, "The band isn't playing in France this week."

But I went out to the road and waited to be picked up until the sunset, and nobody came. I just walked back into the house. No one had showed up. The next day when I confronted the liar—the scammer—he laughed. His friends laughed along with him.

TYPES OF SCAM

Now, these scams can become very big and elaborate. You can get *hedge-fund-sized scams* like *Bernie Madoff's Ponzi scheme*. Mr. Madoff got as many as 37,000[1] people to trust him with their money. Investors thought, "Well, this is a guy on Wall Street and he's very reputable, so why not? Why can't I trust millions of dollars with Bernie Madoff?"

It's still unknown how many billions he scammed his clients out of; however, the judge ordered a $171 billion forfeiture and sentenced Madoff to 150 years in prison—the maximum.[2]

In our new digital age, there are new scams that have to do with cryptocurrency. People have been scammed by *mining scams*—that's where you pay for crypto miners and they're not there or they were there but they closed shop and ran away with your digital coins.

There are *staking scams*—this is where you're supposed to deposit your coins in a wallet and earn interest, but if it's too good to be true, it usually is a scam. They don't give you the high interest and they steal your cryptos.

There are *exchanges* that are scams—you can deposit, you can trade, but you can never withdraw. Their terms and conditions say that they can withhold your funds if for any reason their "Compliance Department" is not satisfied with your account. People whose funds are stolen feel very anguished to be cheated out of their savings.

The scams that are being perpetuated on an unsuspecting world every day are mind-numbing. Oftentimes, scammers have done damage before the ruse is discovered and laws are put in place to protect the public. To expect the government to fix your scam is probably going to take some time. Meanwhile, you've been hit, and there may not be anything you can do about it in the natural. Why? Because the scammers know the industry is unregulated. Their registered address is in a tax haven like Seychelles or offshore in Hong Kong. If they're in a jurisdiction where you could file a lawsuit against them, the scammers rely on the fact that most victims they steal from don't have the money to hire expensive lawyers.

Ironically, scammers prefer to target the poor and vulnerable, not the rich and powerful.

This happens a lot with Nigerian scammers. Kind-hearted people get caught in elaborate, transnational deals. They trust someone who claims to run an orphanage in Africa, and they naively give their banking details to them. Then they are swindled out of their hard-earned savings, or worse, the scammer makes an illegal deposit into your bank account to blame you for a part of their massive, hidden crime.

When your bank account is used for illegal activity, that's the evidence the police have to pursue, so they will go after the wrong person. You, the victim, become mistaken by the authorities for the perpetrator.

You would think the authorities should know better, but they don't. When they accuse the wrong person, they will say they're just "doing their job."

It is so tragic to watch innocent people get scammed.

WHAT CAN YOU DO IF YOU'RE A VICTIM?

There's not much you can do in the natural. I've talked with lawyers and private investigators. Lawyers are expensive. Government agencies are inefficient. Most people find the hurdle too high to pursue a crook across international boundaries. Most people resign themselves to having lost money or property to a scammer.

There is one exception.

In the age of social media, if you're an influencer, you can put a lot of pressure on public scammers. You can expose a known scam if you have a large social following. Make sure you say only what you can prove and not beyond that. There is a risk the scammer could sue you for defamation, but 1) truth is an absolute defense to defamation, and 2) it is unlikely that a scammer would wish to reveal their true identity in court because a career scammer prefers to stay anonymous.

Besides posting a "caveat emptor" (buyer beware) warning on your social media network, you can leave bad reviews on websites like Trustpilot.com. You can petition Apple to remove an app from their App Store if you can demonstrate that the company is acting unethically. You can also petition Google to flag a website with an "unsafe site" label, but Google will not always listen to "little people."

One of my church members was scammed of her life-savings, worth over $300,000. The company was offshore and she found that many people on the Internet complained about the same problem she was facing. In hindsight, she could have avoided her problem by doing the following:

1) check online reviews before buying or investing anything of worth,

2) check for the names of company officers—if they are kept secret, it's a red flag,

3) keep her business and investments in her own country or in related jurisdictions like the United States of America and the Commonwealth countries (nations that respect the rule of law including Australia, Canada, New Zealand, Singapore and the United Kingdom).

Hindsight is 20/20. She did not do any of these, and the online entity she entrusted with her savings was registered offshore with no names of any public officers, so it made it impossible to track down who they were and who was responsible.

Within two weeks of doing what I'm about to tell you, *she recovered all her money.* It may not happen for you as quickly or in the same way, but the point is that you don't have to be powerless. You may not have the influence, the money, or the technological know-how to recover your own losses from a scam artist, but I'm here to tell you, you don't have to feel hopeless or anguished. There is something that you can do if you're a born-again child of God. You just may not know it yet.

In the following chapters, you will learn what to do both spiritually and naturally. You will discover how to find peace and justice once you have been scammed, then you will learn how to avoid scams in the first place. It pains me to see any Christian get scammed. I believe with all my heart, based on the Word of God, that our Heavenly Father has given us the power to do something about it. So let's turn first to the spiritual solution.

You may wish to combine what you learn with a natural solution. For instance, you may seek the help of consumer protection watchdogs, a current affair-type TV show that exposes crooks, private investigators, lawyers, Apple, Google, etc. That's up to you.

But first, as a Christian, you should do *three things* in pursuit of justice and restoration. Follow these three steps as part of your spiritual solution.

Chapter One

TITHER'S RIGHTS

I. MAKE SURE YOU'RE A TITHER.

If you've ever been scammed, believe the Bible and make sure you are a tither. Yes, as a pastor for more than 20 years, I know all the theological excuses. I've heard them all, and they're wrong. This is God's Word. Whether it's in Genesis, Malachi, Matthew or Hebrews, tithing is in God's Word. And God couldn't have made it any simpler for us to do. If you want to make sure that you recover from any cheats or scams, then pay attention to God's Word.

SCAMMING GOD

MALACHI 3:8-11

8 "Will a man rob God? Yet you have robbed Me!

Imagine scamming God! We don't like scammers, but there are people who scam God!

8...But you say, 'In what way have we robbed You?' [His answer...]

In tithes and offerings. [Other translations say "tithes and contributions."]

9 You are cursed with a curse, For you have robbed Me, Even this whole nation.

When unexpected losses happen to you, it's a curse. When people you trust cheat you, it's a curse. One mishap may be random. But a series of strange mishaps should get our attention. Our spiritual alarm system should sound. What should we do?

10 Bring all the tithes into the storehouse, [that's the local church, the place where you get fed spiritually], **That there may be food in My house, And TRY Me now in this** [other translations say "PROVE Me" and "TEST Me." You're allowed to test God in this!]**," Says the Lord of hosts, "If I will not open for you the windows of heaven And pour out for you such blessing That there will not be room enough to receive it.**

11 And I will rebuke the devourer for your sakes, So that he will not destroy the fruit of your ground, Nor shall the vine fail to bear fruit for you in the field," Says the Lord of hosts;

Wow, that's what a lot of people need. They need the Lord Himself to rebuke the scammer, the thief, the liar, the cheater in their life. He said He would rebuke that person or entity for your sake.

So my question is to all those who say *"tithing is not for today,"* is protection from scammers for today? Do you still want God's Hand of Protection for today? Because if you do, the cost of tithing will likely be far less than the cost of getting scammed and being cheated.

It's a very simple formula. I give something that's comparatively small, 10% of my income, in order to be protected from being cheated and losing exorbitantly. Prove Him! It's not something that a pastor or a church made up. God Almighty said, *"You can test Me on this."*

How is God going to solve your injustice? I don't know, but one way or another, He'll make it come back to you if you're a tither because that's His promise. So we confidently say, *"I have tither's rights."* Let's read it again in the King James Version.

MALACHI 3:11-12 (KJV)

11 And I will rebuke the devourer for your sakes, and he shall not destroy the fruits of your ground; neither shall your vine cast her fruit before the time in the field, saith the LORD of hosts.

12 And all nations shall call you blessed: for ye shall be a delightsome land, saith the LORD of hosts.

Would you like that? Instead of being scammed, all the world watching will say, *"You are blessed! I heard you were scammed, but now I see you are blessed! What happened to you?"*

Sometimes tithers don't realize how much protection they have because the bad things the devil planned for them never came to pass. Only in Heaven will we fully appreciate how much the angels of God worked around the clock to prevent the tither from experiencing an accident or a scam that was intended for them.

It will help you to read this verse again in a different version—the English Standard Version:

MALACHI 3:11-12 (ESV)

11 I will rebuke the devourer for you, so that it will not destroy the fruits of your soil, and your vine in the field shall not fail to bear, says the LORD of hosts.

12 Then all nations will call you blessed, for you will be a land of delight, says the LORD of hosts.

Isn't that good? In our ministry, whenever we've met businessmen in trouble, people who've been cheated by business partners of millions of dollars, the first thing we've always told them for decades is "make sure you're a tither."

Some of them have been scammed till they had nothing left, and they said to us, *"I got nothing to tithe."* I told them, *"Well, whatever you're going to use, or whatever you have left, make sure you tithe! Whatever's going to come in in the future, make sure you tithe! Whatever you were robbed of, if you get it back, make sure you tithe!"* That's it. God will even do it on a promise—I call it "on credit."

BLESSED ON CREDIT

You can **receive on credit**. What I mean is, you haven't got anything to give yet, but you make a vow to God to say, *"When it happens, if You deliver me, then I will give You at least 10%."* Hannah, Elkanah's wife, was an infertile woman who received on credit. She did not have a son to dedicate to God's service, but she pledged, "O Lord of hosts, if You will indeed look on the affliction of Your maidservant and remember me, and not forget Your maidservant, but will give Your maidservant a male child, then I will give him to the Lord all the days of his life..." (1 Samuel 1:11).

She had no child to give to God, but she said in effect, "If I had a child, I would dedicate my firstborn son to You." Back then this was no small pledge. It meant giving up her firstborn son (and may be her only child—for who knew that she would have more?) to live away from home, to live in the Temple in Jerusalem, and to serve God in ministry. Not only did God accept her giving on credit, He answered her prayer and made her son the most honored prophet of the land. Samuel would grow up to judge Israel and anoint her first two kings: Saul and David.

I have received on credit many times. I didn't have a thing to give yet, but the moment I pledged to God, my prayer answer came. I received a breakthrough on credit.

One of my church members was scammed of her retirement funds. She invested it in a company that froze her assets when her investment began to increase. They would not let her funds out, and she needed them to fix her teeth. The cost of fixing her teeth in Australia was in excess of $30,000. She had $300,000 tied up in this company.

So she made a pledge, *"Lord, when You release my funds, two-thirds will go to building Your Church, and I will take one-third for fixing my teeth and any retirement needs."* That was a bold pledge. She was offering God something she did not have. Certainly giving God $200,000 and keeping $100,000 was better than losing all of $300,000. People often don't think this. I asked her, *"Are you sure that you have tithed and you don't owe God anything?"* I was confident that she had tithed, but it's important to get people to say it, to release their own faith. There is confidence when you obey God. People who walk in obedience—in God's will—have a stronger faith than those who don't. You will need strong faith to put you through tough times. Weak faith won't last through the trials. The Bible tells us the secret of obtaining prayer answers: knowing God's will and walking in obedience to God's will.

1 JOHN 5:14-15

14 Now this is the confidence that we have in Him, that if we ask anything ACCORDING TO HIS WILL, He hears us.

15 And if we know that He hears us, whatever we ask, WE KNOW that we have the petitions that we have asked of Him.

My church member replied, *"Yes. I've tithed."* She knew God's will and was a doer of it. She was a tither. Therefore she could confidently claim "tither's rights." Plus she vowed two-thirds of the locked funds to God. Don't you think that gives God the Father clear consent to act on her behalf? (A lot of sincere believers haven't given God their consent for Him to intervene, and He isn't rude to intrude. He waits till you consent to be a doer of His will.)

Here was a child of God being cheated, and she was a faith tither and she promised to give on credit. Will not God act on her behalf?

After she made this vow, I had a dream. I woke up in the middle of the night and heard clearly and loudly in my spirit five words:

"THE RESTRICTIONS HAVE BEEN LIFTED"

It was so uplifting that I felt it applied to more than my church member's situation. I felt the restrictions in my own spirit, in my own family, in my own life, had been lifted also! I felt such a freedom I told others about it. Meanwhile, nothing had changed, but I told my church member and we rejoiced by faith. God's Word is good enough for us.

In the natural, it was still frustrating to deal with a company that would delay and not give reasons for what they were doing. When we read online reviews of the company, there were daily complaints from others who could not access their funds. They had support channels on Twitter and Telegram and literally every hour, someone else complained of being scammed. If you looked only at the natural, you would be discouraged. But in our case, my church member had tithed and had made a strong vow, and God spoke, "The restrictions have been lifted."

One week later, her account was unlocked, though her ability to withdraw remained frozen for another 48 hours. After this state of limbo, she was able to recover all her funds. Praise God! Hallelujah!

So many people have made such vows to God, *"Oh Lord, if you get me out of this mess, then I will go to Church every week, I will read the Bible, I will give to Church."* People have made such promises to God, and God came through for them, but they never make good their word. They said, *"If You save me from this, I will serve You,"* and then they go off and serve Mammon, money and the world.

You have to remember those vows. God never forgets.

The moral is: you can make a vow or a pledge, and God will receive it on credit. Nothing's happened yet, you've not given any tithes or offerings yet, but He'll take it on credit and bless you on credit.

I know God's a good God. Many times I didn't have it yet for Him and I said, *"Oh, Lord, if You do it for me, I will do this for You,"* and boom! The answer came. He's that good a God, even our **intention to do it** counts. He says, *"I'll count it!"* But make no foolish vows! Remember your vows and pay them!

Believe it or not, not every pastor tithes. You would think they would, but that's not always true. I know a British pastor who retired and immigrated to America many years ago. He began attending church and became a dear member of the church, and occasionally, the church asked him to preach. He and his family gracefully served in the church, and they made a special effort to reach out to those who were hurting. They were fine Christians in every sense of the world except for one thing: They didn't tithe.

It wasn't because they were poor. The retired pastor drove around in a Mercedes, and they lived in a substantial house on a lake. Then one day the pastor told me he lost $50,000—part of his retirement fund—in a Bernie Madoff-type Ponzi scheme.

While this dear man and his family were my friends and did many good things for the community and the church, they lacked in their devotion to God in the area of tithing.

Was it mere coincidence they lost all of that money? I don't believe so. As the rabbis say, "Coincidence is not a kosher word." God loved this preacher too much to leave him in his sin. He loves us too much not to correct and discipline us when we are wrong. Remember, God is preparing us to serve Him in His eternal kingdom with all our hearts, souls, minds, and strength. We may be magnificent in many areas, but if we lack in the area of tithing, it will eventually catch up with us.

Remember the story of the rich man who came to Jesus thinking he was ready for eternal life, yet he was unwilling to part with his money when Jesus asked him? What did Jesus say about him? "It is hard for a rich man to enter the kingdom of heaven" (Matthew 19:23). Don't be like the rich man. Give to God because you created nothing and He created everything. God created the universe to obey the law of the tithe. His Word says that He protects the tither; He is not obligated to protect the disobedient. People don't like to hear that, but when tragedy strikes, it is not God's fault. He wants to restore you if you have suffered loss and give you more than you had before.

Chapter Two

SEVEN-FOLD RETURN

2. DEAL WITH THE DEVIL, NOT THE PERSON.

Too many times we make our fight with people when the real enemy we should be fighting is the old devil. You may say, "But it was my relative who stole my inheritance." Yes and no. That relative was a vessel Satan used to get to you. Satan likes to use people close to you because it hurts more.

But rather than dealing with the relative directly, it is better to deal first with the spiritual influence behind that person. According to the Bible, whatever the devil stole, he must return seven-fold. Make sure that you pray that **whatever the devil stole, he must return seven-fold.** You can pray it just like that. Why? Because it's in the Bible.

PROVERBS 6:30-31 (ESV)

30 People do not despise a thief if he steals to satisfy his appetite when he is hungry,

31 but if he is caught, he will pay sevenfold; he will give all the goods of his house.

Whatever the devil stole, whoever the devil used to steal from you, however the devil stole, he **must repay seven-fold**. It doesn't have to come the way you imagine, it doesn't have to come the way you think, but **it must come**.

So you calculate what was stolen from you, and then you **make a demand in the spirit**. You say,

*"Satan, no more! You don't do this to me anymore **in Jesus' Name**. You're going to pay me back seven-fold. You're going to be sorry that you took from me because it's going to hurt you seven times worse."*

YOU ARE ALLOWED TO PRAY THIS WAY IF...

1. You're a born-again child of God
2. You're a tither. You've not stolen from God. So don't scam God yourself!
3. You believe Proverbs chapter 6 verse 31.

It's important to deal with the spiritual powers first before you confront the natural parties. If you focus on the people, you will feel bad and hopeless. You will lose sleep thinking about why So-and-So scammed you, how you could have avoided it, how you can recover it, and are they going to get away with it.

There's no point to second guess yourself after the fact because you can't turn back time and even the smartest people in the world get scammed. Robert Kiyosaki is the #1 financial education author in the English-speaking world, yet was scammed by a gold mining deal.[1] The Chinese government promised him a license to mine gold if he and his business partner, Frank Crerie, took the Chinese gold mining company public on the Toronto Stock Exchange.

They did, and when the company struck gold, rather than getting rich, the Chinese Communist state confiscated their gold mine. Their excuse? The same as was used in Argentina when the state nationalized private mines. That foreigners like Kiyosaki weren't taking care of the environment.

How ironic coming from the world's largest polluter! When you're scammed by the state, who do you turn to? Could you have written better contracts, hired better lawyers, signed with better partners, promise to be better than China about the environment? No, no, no and no. There's nothing in the natural even an expert could do.

Rather than focusing on the people and ignoring the devil, the Bible tells us to first focus on the devil and ignore the people involved. There's no point feeling bad about yourself and there's certainly no point feeling bad for the devil. He is corrupt to the core and irredeemable for eternity. Jesus called him a thief, murderer and destroyer.

JOHN 10:10

The thief does not come except to steal, and to kill, and to destroy. I have come that they may have life, and that they may have it more abundantly.

Anybody that steals, kills and destroys comes from the devil, not God. The devil may use a human to plot evil, just like God will use a human to carry out His plan on the earth. I want you to observe how Jesus dealt with the Pharisees who constantly opposed Him and accused Him.

From the start of Jesus' ministry in Israel, the Pharisee became jealous of Jesus. They didn't know what to do with His popularity, they couldn't compete with His sermons, and they certainly had nothing to compare to His miracles and healings. He was a blessing to ordinary people, but a threat to the religious establishment.

They tried to catch Him in His words, but Jesus always had an answer that they couldn't anticipate. They were normally successful at entrapping people.

MATTHEW 22:15-17

15 Then the Pharisees went and plotted how they might entangle Him in His talk.

16 And they sent to Him their disciples with the Herodians, saying, "Teacher, we know that You are true, and teach the way of God in truth; nor do You care about anyone, for You do not regard the person of men.

17 Tell us, therefore, what do You think? Is it

lawful to pay taxes to Caesar, or not?"

This was a "damned if you, damned if you don't" type of question. If Jesus answered that Jews should pay Roman taxes, then He would be seen as a Roman sympathizer, appeaser or compromiser by His Jewish audience. If Jesus answered that Jews shouldn't pay taxes to the Romans, then He would be perceived as treasonous, rebellious or seditious by the Romans. Either answer, the Jews had Him...or so they thought.

People who scam you usually try to make you think that you have less options than you do. How did Jesus answer?

MATTHEW 22:18-21

18 But Jesus perceived their wickedness, and said, "Why do you test Me, you hypocrites?

19 Show Me the tax money." So they brought Him a denarius.

20 And He said to them, "Whose image and inscription is this?"

21 They said to Him, "Caesar's." And He said to them, "Render therefore to Caesar the things that are Caesar's, and to God the things that are God's."

22 When they had heard these words, they marveled, and left Him and went their way.

The Pharisees failed at entrapment several times, but they did not give up. They were very embittered about

Jesus. For four long years they followed His ministry not to learn from Him, but to find fault with Him. You probably know people like that. Unfortunately, because you and I are sinners, they will be able to find some of our faults. No one is perfect, no one except Jesus.

Jesus was blameless. He was sinless, which made the scammers' mission all the more frustrating for them. When they couldn't defeat Jesus in a fair debate, they did what evil people usually do next: they threw baseless and outrageous charges at Jesus, bolstered by false witnesses.

They also reported Jesus to the Roman authorities, believing that they could leverage Roman fears of an uprising on the outskirts of the empire. After all, Jesus was being heralded by the Jewish people as their Messiah. The rabbis were happy to clarify that one meaning of the word "Messiah" could mean a rival king. That was a political interpretation of Scripture. A Savior to the Jews was a challenger to Caesar. Experts of the law, as the Pharisees were, have a way of twisting words to suit their case.

Yes, there was some truth that Jesus came as the King of the Jews, but because His Kingdom would not start out as political, He constantly resisted attempts to spread His fame, to make His miracles known, and to be crowned as a king. This explains many Scriptures that people don't understand.

JOHN 6:14-15 [This incident happened after Jesus multiple the five loaves and two fishes to feed 5000 people...]

14 Then those men, when they had seen the

sign that Jesus did, said, "This is truly the Prophet who is to come into the world."

[Another name for the Messiah is "the Prophet" whom Moses promised would come after him to save Israel, a prophecy found in Deuteronomy 18:15.]

15 Therefore when Jesus perceived that they were about to come and take Him by force to make Him king, He departed again to the mountain by Himself alone.

His reaction was inexplicable if He wanted to be famous or powerful in a worldly sense. He kept downplaying His Divinity and His Kingship, preferring to call Himself "the Son of Man" even though He accepted worship as "the Son of God." When Thomas worshipped Him as, "My Lord, my God," Jesus did not correct Thomas (John 20:28). Jesus accepted the disciples' recognition that He is the Lord of the Universe, the Creator God come in the flesh.

Jesus acted like God, talked like God, and accepted worship as God, yet He constantly downplayed His Divinity. He did not fit the picture the Pharisees painted of Him to others.

JOHN 18:36-37

36 Jesus answered, "My kingdom is not of this world. If My kingdom were of this world, My servants would fight, so that I should not be delivered to the Jews; but now My kingdom is not from here."

37 Pilate therefore said to Him, "Are You a king then?" Jesus answered, "You say rightly that I am a king. For this cause I was born, and for this cause I have come into the world, that I should bear witness to the truth. Everyone who is of the truth hears My voice."

Their accusation was that Jesus said He was a rival king. Although Jesus presented no threat to Caesar, there was enough ammunition to convict Him. There is usually some truth mixed in with lies when you're dealing with a scammer.

Jesus then went through six unjust trials in what we would call kangaroo courts or Star Chambers. This means that before the trial started and the evidence was shown, the authorities had leaned one way and the outcome had been predetermined, yet everyone went through the rigmarole of appearing legitimate, and they played along to get to the intended goal of hurting Jesus. It was a ruse, a scam of the highest sort.

With this background, what I want you to see is how Jesus dealt with the scammers. Most of the time, you should ignore unreasonable people. You're not going to be able to reason with them. But you do have to fight the spirit behind them.

JOHN 8:44

44 You are of your father the devil, and the desires of your father you want to do. He was a murderer from the beginning, and does not stand

in the truth, because there is no truth in him. When he speaks a lie, he speaks from his own resources, for he is a liar and the father of it.

Jesus went straight to the source of conflict: the devil. The devil will influence humans to do devilish things. His nature is to lie, steal, kill and destroy, so those under his power do the same. The devil is the father of lies, which means he is the father of scams.

Jesus continued...

45 But because I tell the truth, you do not believe Me.

46 Which of you convicts Me of sin? And if I tell the truth, why do you not believe Me?

47 He who is of God hears God's words; therefore you do not hear, because you are not of God."

Jesus blamed the devil for the Pharisees' behavior—their conniving, stubbornness, hate and resistance to the truth. You can also blame the devil for what scammers did to you. It is often fruitless to think about the human agent the devil uses to hurt you. *"Why did they do this to me? How could they do this to me? Are they going to get away with it?"* These questions weaken your faith and disempower you because they don't always have answers. If you had the answers, you probably wouldn't have been scammed. Why lose precious sleep over it?

One way to know that you're in faith is that you can go

to sleep at night. Cast your worries and cares on the Lord and let the Lord work it out even in your sleep.

1 PETER 5:7

7 casting all your care upon Him, for He cares for you.

PROVERBS 3:24

24 When you lie down, you will not be afraid; Yes, you will lie down and your sleep will be sweet.

Now that you know the devil is to blame for influencing people's bad behavior, the "thief has been caught" according to Proverbs 6:31. When he is caught stealing, you can demand that he repay you seven-fold in Jesus' name. The people who stole from you may not know it, but they will repay much more than seven-fold, because they are on the path to hell if they don't repent. Let God deal with troublemakers. But it's up to you to take authority over the devil and tell him to stop stealing from you in Jesus' Name!

JOHN 16:23-24

23 "And in that day you will ask Me nothing. Most assuredly, I say to you, whatever you ask the Father IN MY NAME He will give you.

24 Until now you have asked nothing IN MY NAME. Ask, and you will receive, that your joy may be full.

Chapter Three

BIBLICAL JUSTICE

3. STOCK UP ON SCRIPTURES ABOUT JUSTICE.

Waiting for Restoration

What should you do while you are waiting for vindication and restoration? What I would do, because God cares so much about justice, is I would stock up on Scriptures about Justice.

If you build your faith on only one Scripture, you're going to easily waver or topple over. Your faith won't be stable. Any one-legged chair is unstable. Faith is like a chair that needs 3, or better yet 4, Scriptures to stand on. When I ask people, "Do you believe God wants to do this for you?" they always tell me, "Yes." When I check the quality of their faith (a pastor has to check like a doctor has to diagnose you), "What Scripture are you standing on?" they usually say *"Ask and you shall receive,"* which is not a Scripture per se, but a paraphrase of Matthew 7:7-8.

This is a general principle, but it's not a specific promise for your situation. You're going to need something more than that when you're going through the storms of life. You're going to need at least 3 to 4 Scriptures that you meditate on—that you're confident about. Find those Scriptures. Put them on your refrigerator, put them on your bedroom wall, put them in your toilet, put them wherever it will help you. Make sure you stock up on some good Scriptures about Justice.

I've compiled 8 Scriptures about restoration you can use right away. I don't see other Christian authors putting together Scripture prayer books on justice. They put out prayer books on love and healing, and those things are great, but I've not seen a Scripture prayer book for justice.

Our keynote verse was Deuteronomy 32. This is our foundation for justice.

DEUTERONOMY 32:4 (ESV)

4 "The Rock, his work is perfect, for ALL his ways are JUSTICE. A God of faithfulness and without iniquity, just and upright is he.

We know God cares about justice and He cares about bringing justice to the Earth, especially for His children. Now that you have come into the Family of Justice, you can invoke His authority for justice, you can sue for justice in the Courts of Heaven. So which Scriptures are you going to use when you pray about things that have been stolen from you? I would use the following. You can pick whatever you want to use from the Bible; these are just my best eight:

1ˢᵗ **Scripture:**

JAMES 5:4 (ESV)

4 Behold, the wages of the laborers who mowed your fields, which you kept back by fraud, are crying out against you, and the cries of the harvesters have reached the ears of the Lord of hosts.

If something has been promised to you, but the promiser is keeping it back, you can cry out to God. And God says, *"I am listening to the cries of My people"* because *"the laborer is worthy of his wages,"* (1 Timothy 5:18). The Bible teaches that if you worked hard for something, you deserve to be paid.

It's a strange thing to me that there are Christians who don't want to pay for anything. They write on my YouTube channel nearly every time we invite people to join online church. They comment, *"Oh, this church, they charge to be on online church,"* In order for them to make that comment, they had to have just watched a free video! They just listened to a free video and they're complaining. And my answer is always the same. There's no need to go deep into theology because some people's minds are closed anyway. Jesus is our example and He purchased things. Jesus sent His disciples to go buy food (John 4:8). He told his disciples to buy a sword (Luke 22:36). He told his disciples to buy gold, clothes and eye salve (Revelation 3:18). Notice Jesus didn't give them out for free. When Judas left the last supper, the other disciples assumed Jesus had said to him, "BUY those things we need for the feast" (John 13:29). It was a regular habit for them to pay and not expect free stuff just because they're people of faith.

LUKE 22:36

Then He said to them, "But now, he who has a money bag, let him take it, and likewise a knapsack; and he who has no sword, let him sell his garment and BUY one.

REVELATION 3:18

"I counsel you to BUY from Me gold refined in the fire, that you may be rich; and white garments, that you may be clothed, that the shame of your nakedness may not be revealed; and anoint your eyes with eye salve, that you may see."

Jesus taught that the foolish were not willing to pay for things. When they needed oil, they begged the wise virgins for essential supply. But the wise answered the foolish, "No, lest there should not be enough for us and you; but go rather to those who sell, and BUY for yourselves" (Matthew 25:9).

So my answer is not to get into intricate theology because it's so absolutely clear—God believes in the free market. God believes that the laborer is worthy of his wages. I just tell Christian who want everything free, *"We're not a communist ministry."* If you expect everything to be redistributed for free, equally to everybody, with no payment —that's called communism—that's Satan's system.

On this planet, we put value on things and we pay for whatever we value. You're not forced to buy anything. You're not forced to support or subscribe to anything from Discover Church. It's a choice. It's funny to me that Christians don't think twice to spend their money on the Internet, on their phone, on basically all the things of the world—Netflix, Disney+, Amazon Prime. Oh, Christians don't mind spending on all that, but to contribute $20 to have access to a high-quality presentation of the Word of God 4 times a month, plus Bible courses and a Christian community, some of them complain. We have the same costs as all these seculars companies. So you know what? I just confess to such Christians, "I'm not a communist. I don't support communism. I support the free market."

If you work hard, you deserve to be paid. And those who receive income should be responsible to pay tithes, taxes and give offerings to help others. We should have that as a Christian economic model. Everybody who works hard deserves to be paid. And if you worked hard on something and you were not paid, you can cry out to God. You can cry out and God says, *"I'm listening"* because God is not a communist.

God doesn't say, *"Well, I kind of thought you had too much money, so I took your money and I gave it to somebody else,"* He doesn't do that. God's not going to do that to you. Hard work has value that should be paid.

When people don't pay us, we feel it's unfair, but when we don't pay other people, we might feel we have a justification. You need to examine your own life in light of this Scripture. Have you withheld payment to anyone? Do you pay your bills in full and on time? If you're a boss, what would your employees say about you behind your back? Do you give bonuses that reflect people's excellence or extra work? What would your own family say about your level of generosity?

An author friend of mine hired someone through a third party to narrate one of her books so it could become an audiobook. After working with the narrator, my friend realized the person she hired could not fulfill her contractual obligations. Two months past the deadline, the author contacted the third party who held the contract to terminate the relationship with the hired narrator. Because the narrator missed the deadline, the author was under no obligation to pay her anything. Despite that, the author paid the narrator a portion of the money she expected had she finished the project.

PROVERBS 14:12 (NLT)
There is a path before each person that seems right, but it ends in death.

While earthly standards might seem good enough, we should walk according to a higher standard, especially when dealing with another Christian. It may be your right not to pay them anything, but then a brother or sister might accuse you of being cheap, not being fair, or shortchanging them. Why give them such an opportunity to ruin your good reputation? A brother or sister might even say you scammed them despite the fact you didn't under the terms of the contract.

1 CORINTHIANS 6:7-8

7 Now therefore, it is already an utter failure for you that you go to law against one another. Why do you not rather accept wrong? Why do you not rather let yourselves be cheated?

8 No, you yourselves do wrong and cheat, and you do these things to your brethren!

Sometimes it's better to cut your losses and leave a good example. This way you remove any chance of people slamming your Christian faith or accusing you of injustice. Sometimes it's more profitable to be a fool for God's sake. Your reward will not be from man, but from God who witnesses your generosity. Many a times, a Christian's generosity has brought a lost soul into God's kingdom. Never underestimate the power of paying people on time, in full, and even when you don't think they deserve it.

2nd Scripture:

LEVITICUS 19:11, 13 (ESV)

11 "You shall not steal; you shall not deal falsely; you shall not lie to one another.

Scammers do all that—they steal, they lie, they deal falsely.

13 "You shall not oppress your neighbor or rob him. The wages of a hired worker shall not remain with you all night until the morning.

Imagine living in God's system. Currently a lot of people work and get paid once a month. At most, you might get paid once a week. In God's economy, He told the Israelites, "Don't even keep the workers' wages overnight. Owe no man anything." When you go to sleep, you might not wake up tomorrow. Make sure you paid everything, then go to sleep every night owing nothing. Well, that's totally anti-communism! That's God's economy.

Keeping something from someone for too long is a kind of theft. Delaying to pay your obligation is a kind of theft. The Lord instructs us, don't do it!

3rd Scripture:

PROVERBS 20:17 (ESV)
17 Bread gained by deceit is sweet to a man, but afterward his mouth will be full of gravel.

I like to pray that, ***"Oh Lord, fill the mouth of every scammer with gravel."*** How are you going to talk with gravel in your mouth? You won't be talking so well. How are you going to talk when the authorities come down hard on you and investigate you for scamming people? They'll put you to jail. You'll get gravel in your mouth before a judge.

4th Scripture:

I like this one a lot. Micah chapter 2. If you like any of these Scriptures, write it down, type it up, print it out, make it pretty if you want—just use it!

MICAH 2:1-3 (NIV)

1 Woe to those who plan iniquity, to those who plot evil on their beds! At morning's light they carry it out because it is in their power to do it.

Scammers cheat you because they think they can get away with it. They do it because they think you are powerless against them. I guarantee you, you're not powerless as a Christian, and you're not powerless as a group of people. You just have to find other people if you've been scammed as a group. You've got to band together and come against a scammer.

Scammers can act quite nonchalant about cheating and hurting other people, but if you walk with God, He will bring other people around you to protect you.

A Christian friend of mine shared this story with me. One day an arborist stopped by her house and left his business card on the door which read, "Heaven's Tree Service."

It was at a time when she needed some yard work done, but she didn't have time to find someone to do the work.

When she read the name on the card, her first thought was, "Oh, God has sent someone to me. How convenient." She hired the man on the spot.

The first day the arborist was there, her beloved cat died. Then she remembered how for years she had dreamed about making a pet memorial garden on the side of her house. She asked the arborist if he could clear that part of the yard along with the other work he was doing.

As the day progressed, the man kept coming back wanting more money. Because he had already started the work and she was distracted mourning about her cat, she kept giving the man the money he asked for to get the job done. All the while, she had the feeling she was being scammed, but in her grief, she didn't have the strength to confront the scammer or to say no.

My friend said she listened from inside the house as the arborist spoke harshly to his day laborers—hirelings from the local homeless shelter. The tree expert claimed he was giving them experience so they could get a job as an arborist. By the end of the day, the woman no longer liked the man and felt sorry she had hired him.

When the work was all done, she felt used, realizing she had been fooled by his knowledge of the Bible, his past life as a pastor, and the name of the company—Heaven's Tree Service. She had trusted him merely because he presented himself as a Christian. What could she do now? He had taken advantage of her during a time of extraordinary pain and unexpected loss.

The next day, one of the homeless men who had worked for the arborist rang the doorbell. Reluctantly, she went to the door, prepared to tell him that she didn't need any more yard work done.

However, he wouldn't talk to her at the door. He insisted she come outside to the area that was cleared the day before and tell him how much she had paid to his boss. After going through her checkbook and calculating the total, the day worker held up some discarded garden materials. "He got this from his yard. It isn't even new." The clincher was when he played a recording on his phone from the night before. The tree man was laughing. "Oh, it's fine. She won't notice. If she does, we can redo it later. She has lots of money."

All my friend could do was think back to the warning signs she had ignored. Just because someone says he's a Christian doesn't mean you should trust him in business. She determined to learn from this eye-opening experience.

The homeless man turned out to be a messenger sent from God. To make it up to her, he took the small amount of money his boss had paid him and went to the store, bought flowers for her, and planted them for free.

"I just want to make it up to you, Ma'am," the homeless man said. "It's the least I can do."

While she never got money back from the arborist, God used a homeless man to bless her and used her to bless the homeless man. Sometimes help arrives in ways we don't expect. For her, she did not get a dollar-for-dollar return after injustice had been perpetrated, yet God's ways touched her heart at a deeper level than an earthly refund can. For the homeless man, he had a chance to act richer than his boss, and did it. His reward will be greater than the ex-pastor's rewards.

When we are cheated, it's hard to see the greater good that comes out of it. But from God's perspective, He is ultimately working all things out for good.

> **2 They covet fields and seize them, and houses, and take them. They defraud people of their homes, they rob them of their inheritance.**

Some scammers knock on your door. Some scammers are in your family! An inheritance was supposed to go some way but they stole it. I know a father who stole the inheritance of his own Down Syndrome daughter. She needed medical attention but he wouldn't pay. He just used the money for his own properties and ignored other family members' pleas to give his daughter her inheritance. When it's your family, you can be so angry and powerless at the same time because you don't generally want to accuse your family or take them to court.

I've seen these situations as a pastor, and I can tell you, nobody gets away with anything. It comes back to them one way or another. The Lord says, "Vengeance is Mine, I will repay, says the Lord," (Hebrews 10:30, Romans 12:19).

Remember #1 make sure you're a tither; #2 make sure you pray that whatever the devil stole, he must return seven-fold, then #3 be at peace, stock up on some Scriptures about God's wonderful Justice! He is a just God. He is a good God. Let's continue to the next verse in Micah chapter 2.

3 Therefore, the LORD says: "I am planning disaster against this people, from which you cannot save yourselves. You will no longer walk proudly, for it will be a time of calamity.

That's how it feels when you're scammed: you don't feel you can save yourself, you can't do anything to bring back what was stolen from you. But the Lord says, *"I am planning disaster against this people."* Now don't rejoice at that, but as surely as He is the Savior of the world, He is planning disaster for scammers.

5th Scripture:

PROVERBS 10:2-3 (God's Word)
2 Treasures gained dishonestly profit no one, but righteousness rescues from death.
3 The LORD will not allow a righteous person to starve, but he intentionally ignores the desires of a wicked person.

The topic of prayer is not as simple as people think. Did you ever hear that God will ignore some people's prayers? Most people don't realize that. Everybody thinks prayer is simple: "I throw up a wish, and I should get it. I ignore God most of the time. I defraud and scam other people. I hurt people with harsh words, and suddenly, I have a need, so I'm just going to throw a prayer request out, and God is supposed to answer me on demand." No, prayer doesn't work that way. Prayer is not as simple as you think.

There are some strict rules and guidelines for prayer. If you want to learn more about different rules for different prayers, I suggest my series on the 9 types of prayer found in the New Testament.[1] When you meet the conditions laid out in the Bible, then prayer become effective.

I like Proverbs chapter 10 verse 3. God will intentionally ignore the desires of a wicked person. May He ignore the prayers of scammers!

6th Scripture:

PROVERBS 13:22

22 A good man leaves an inheritance to his children's children, But the wealth of the sinner is stored up for the righteous.

For generations Christians have heard about the prophecy of the "great wealth transfer." Christians will be freed up to pursue God's ministry without financial limitations. Someone once said that every revival starts with prayer and ends with lack of funding. The world doesn't have a problem expending billions of dollars on failed green projects, ugly modern art, and transportation projects that go nowhere and never get finished.[2] [3] [4] [5]

Why shouldn't God's servants be able to build churches, schools, hospitals, orphanages, without any financial pressure?

We haven't been able to because, for far too long, the

wealth transfer has been going in the opposite direction: from Christians to the world! Christians don't mind paying for the world's internet, the world's social media, the world's online shopping, to name a few expenses. Christians used to be the discoverers and inventors of the world, which brought great wealth into the Kingdom and funded past revivals, churches and denominations— inventors and discoverers like Michael Faraday, Gregor Mendel, Isaac Newton, John Dalton, Florence Nightingale, George Washington Carver, and Samuel Morse.

Contrary to God's will, we have given up Kingdom wealth to enrich the world's corporations. On top of that, Christians lose their precious savings to online scammers like fake Nigerian orphanages.

Until Christians awaken to what they should do with great wealth for God's Kingdom, then sinners are called to "store up" the wealth for the righteous. This "storing up" process seems to be part of God's plan. Sinners are keeping the wealth for the benefit of a generation of believers who will know what to do with a massive release of wealth.

Is there a Biblical example for this? Indeed there is in Exodus. When the Israelites left Egypt under the leadership of Moses, God commanded the Jews to take gold, silver and clothing from the Egyptians.

EXODUS 3:21-22

21 "And I will give this people favor in the sight of the Egyptians; and it shall be, when you go, that you shall not go empty-handed.

22 "But every woman shall ask of her

neighbor, namely, of her who dwells near her house, articles of silver, articles of gold, and clothing; and you shall put them on your sons and on your daughters. So you shall plunder the Egyptians."

Who created this ancient wealth? The Jewish slaves! Little did they know that they were creating wealth for their own future. Why did God allow the Egyptians to store up the wealth? Because when believers get wealth instantly, they often spend it instantly.

God's plan was not for them to become wealthy and use it all for themselves. God wanted them to do something with that wealth that had been accumulated and released the right time. God had His own plans and purposes. What was it? He told Moses the purpose of the wealth shortly after they left Egypt.

EXODUS 25:1-8

1 Then the Lord spoke to Moses, saying:

2 "Speak to the children of Israel, that they BRING Me an OFFERING. From everyone who gives it willingly with his heart you shall take My offering.

3 And this is the offering which you shall take from them: GOLD, SILVER, and bronze;

4 blue, purple, and scarlet thread, fine linen, and goats' hair;

5 ram skins dyed red, badger skins, and acacia wood;

6 oil for the light, and spices for the anointing oil and for the sweet incense;

7 onyx stones, and stones [gemstones] to be set in the ephod and in the breastplate.

8 And let them MAKE Me a SANCTUARY, that I may dwell among them.

Four hundred years of wealth had been stored up for the generation that would build God a "*mishkan*," the Hebrew word for God's dwelling place on Earth. Moses used a portion of that wealth to build the Tabernacle where God's presence dwelt with man.

Do you believe we are that generation called to build God's church—God's embassy on Earth? I do because the world has never had greater needs, the church has never had greater opportunities, and the devil has never had less time. The day of Christians losing money to the world and feeling powerless financially is over. The Lord has always wanted us to be wealthy enough to leave an inheritance to our children and our children's children. Imagine being able to fund the construction of your local church or online church, and also leave a house—one for each of your children and one for each of your grandchildren. For this promise to come to pass, the wealth of the oppressors, thieves and scammers must be returned to the believers.

7th Scripture:

You probably know this Scripture already, but have not applied it to scammers.

GALATIANS 6:7 (NIV)

7 Do not be deceived: God cannot be mocked. A man reaps what he sows.

When you believe God's Word, you can go to bed at night. You know that fraudsters will not get away with it because the Bible says so. *Stop worrying about it.* Worry is a sin anyway. Jesus said so (Matthew 6:25-34).

Everybody has met people who think it's okay to trick and deceive other people. I met them as a 15-year-old boy in southern France. As a young man, I thought, "What's the point of doing that? What's the point of scamming somebody about a little concert?" I learned early on that there are real scammers in the world. Not only that, they're going to get more elaborate, they're going to get smarter, and they're going to get more deceptive as they get older. This is one of the hidden blessings of death. Death did not exist when people were not sinners. Death came by sin. Sinners should not live forever because they get so darn good at sinning. It's the mercy of God that Adam and Eve died, and the children of Adam will all finally die, because if you leave sinners around for two or three hundred years, they can steal a lot of wealth, they can accumulate a lot of power, and they can abuse a lot of people. God does not allow any man to sin forever. Every man reaps what he sows, and the wages of his sin is death (Romans 6:23, Galatians 6:6-7).

I know the scammers don't think about it, but the biggest problem they face is that unless they repent, they're not going to go to Heaven. I've seen guys with tattoos of the Virgin Mary on their arm, and they're scamming people. They'll wear a crucifix on their chest, and they're scamming people. They'll show up to church on Christmas and Easter, but every other day, they live like the devil. The Bible says clearly, if you're a scammer, you're not going to see God, you're not going to go to Heaven, you're not going to be with any of the saints, and you're not going to see any of your wonderful mothers or fathers or aunties or or uncles, or anyone else who's lived for God in your family line. You're going to be isolated and punished forever, and that's the worst part of being a thief. I don't know if they get that, but it's the Bible truth.

8th Scripture:

1 CORINTHIANS 6:9-10 (GNT)
9 Surely you know that the wicked will not possess God's Kingdom.

Surely you know, stealing a few dollars is not worth losing an eternity. Surely you know!

9 Do not fool yourselves; people who are immoral or who worship idols or are adulterers or homosexual perverts
10 or who steal or are greedy or are drunkards or who slander others or are thieves—none of these will possess God's Kingdom.

The scammers are in great danger according to

Scripture. You want to warn them not to risk it. You want to pray they don't go to hell over money.

When a person scams a believer—a tithing believer—it will not go well for them in this life because God defends the tither. He rebukes the scammer. You have His Word on it in Malachi chapter 3.

God hates injustice. I hate injustice. As long as I have breath, we're going to fight injustice on this planet. There are so many issues of justice. Abortion is one big issue that true Christians take a strong stance on. A lot of fine believers have been on that battlefront defending innocent babies, and we're fighting it still. But this one, adult injustice, is one that not a lot of Christians deal with. You can see it's in the Bible. As much as we fight abortion and substance abuse, we should fight scams and thefts, and the slander and defamation that often come with them.

You can see that God has given you power to do something about injustice. Believe the Scriptures and act on them! Take authority over the devil whom Jesus called the thief and the father of lies. If you're a born-again believer, you have the right to break his power in the Name of Jesus.

Make sure you close the spiritual door to the devil if you've left a door open by withholding the tithe! Close that door! The tithe is not 8%, 9%, or 9.9%, it's 10%. Do it the way God says. Pay the full tithe to Him and close that door, then follow these steps I gave you.

You are going to have some good victories. Please share your stories of victory with me. This is why we learn about justice, so that you can experience restoration and vindication. We're not learning the Bible just for the afterlife. You're not going to need justice in the afterlife. You're not going to need justice in Heaven. Why are all these Scriptures here? For you, for now.

But until now you didn't activate it, you didn't believe it. Why? It is partly the fault of us preachers. We didn't preach it. Today, you've heard it. You've read it. I believe your faith has gotten stronger, and now you know what to do.

First, you will do all you can in the natural to avoid scams—that's the focus of our next chapter.

Then you will do all you can to pray God's justice be done in your situation—that's the focus of our last two chapters. The final chapter is a mini prayerbook of the best Scriptures on restoration from injustice. You will want to revisit this chapter of prayers from time to time, as often as you'd like a handy reference to God's Word when you pray.

∼

Chapter Four

PRACTICAL TIPS TO AVOID SCAMS

SCAMMING HAS BECOME A PROFESSIONAL, FULL-TIME industry since our lives and personal data have gone online. If you won a reward online or are offered an online job that will pay you highly for little effort, you are probably being scammed. The general principle you should follow is, "If it seems too good to be true, it probably is."

The majority of scammers are "professionals" and career criminals without a conscience. They know exactly what they are doing and have virtually perfected the art of cheating. Most of us think that scammers target only the vulnerable, the greedy or people who struggle with technology, but that is not true. There's no boundary as to whom they will target. If you don't know what to look out for, you run a higher risk of falling victim to a scam. To not be scammed, you have to be at least one step ahead of them!

MATTHEW 10:16

"Behold, I send you out as sheep in the midst of wolves. Therefore be wise as serpents and harmless as doves.

While it's our role to stand firm on the Scriptures and follow the three steps I outlined as the spiritual solution to scams, God also wants us to be wise while we live in this fallen world. Here are some common frauds and scams and how to prevent them.

CREDIT/ DEBIT CARD SCAMS

This is one of the most common frauds that happens to people. They see a charge on their credit card statements that they did not authorize, then they realize that they've been scammed.

One of my church members is a fraud detective. She is a 'Loss Prevention Advisor' to the largest pharmacy chain in Australia. She has caught syndicates who use stolen electronic cards to make purchases both in store and online. Here's how they work:

Some of them walk into stores with a "shopping list" of the exact goods they're supposed to steal. They select goods worth up to thousands of dollars, pretend to tap their card for payment onto the electronic payment machine and then tell the cashier that their tap service isn't working. They then proceed to key in their credit card number manually on the pin-pad. Of course it's not their own card numbers, but a memorized stolen card numbers. When the transaction is approved, they exit the store happily with the goods. Two victims are created here: the store where goods were stolen and the original card holder whose card was charged.

The scammers also go online to make large purchases with a stolen card and then send the package to a vacant house or unused commercial building. Someone will then pick up the package. These goods are then either sold online or physically for cash. One time, the church member said one of the crooks was caught red-handed with a "shopping list" of the exact goods he was supposed to steal!

What can you do to reduce your risk of credit card fraud?

- Be diligent to check your bank account and credit card statements regularly to ensure there is no unauthorized spending. I recommend at least weekly.
- When discarding your credit card, cut it up in pieces and throw them into different bins and/or on different days. You'll be surprise how people scour through rubbish to see what they can find!
- Don't save your credit card details in any website—even trusted retail websites. It's advisable to save your card details in your own memory than any online sites. You may think it's convenient when you are shopping online, but

saving your details on a webstore makes it easier for hackers to retrieve your details.

- When entering your credit card PIN (personal identity number), use your other hand to cover the buttons as you enter your PIN. Did you know that high-definition security cameras these days can easily zoom in and capture your exact PIN as you key them in? All it takes is one crooked employee in need of money to bring you a lot of hassle.
- If you lose your wallet or credit card, call your bank immediately to cancel the cards and also make a police report (especially if you lose your ID cards to avoid identity theft).
- Put limits on your cards where possible. This will reduce the risk of large amounts of funds being lost.
- Find out if your bank has a notification service where they contact you immediately via call or text if there is a suspicious or flagged transaction.

Not every suspicious charge is a scam. If you see a surprise charge on your credit card statement, you should firstly go through your receipts (online or hardcopy) and ensure that you definitely did not make a purchase. At Discover Church, we occasionally receive chargebacks from banks claiming the card holder did not authorize the payment, but in fact, they made a recurring donation or subscription but forgot about it.

If you are certain you did not make the purchase, you can attempt to contact the retailer or the business who charged you. Sometimes you will not recognize a business name because they have a trading name (public-facing name) that's different from their bank account name (registered or legal name). If you recognize the business name, try and resolve the issue with them. Sometimes there are genuine errors like duplicate charges—they are not necessarily scamming you. Ideally you should contact the business the same day you see an unauthorized charge. There is no reason to wait. If it is not resolved by the end of the same business day or you still have suspicions that it's a fraud, **call your bank immediately!**

Inform them of the unauthorized charge and tell them you want to do a chargeback. A responsible bank will immediately cancel your current card and issue you a new one. Cancelling your card may cause some inconvenience, but it's the safest way to protect yourself against fraudsters. They will usually do more than one charge to maximize their opportunity. A reputable bank should also give you an immediate refund while they are investigating your case.

BUSINESS SCAMS

If you own a business, you can put in place some measures to decrease your risk of fraudulent transactions. If your business has large transactions online, you should incorporate fraud protection software such as Forter and Kount into your online payment platform. These softwares are intelligent enough to block bad actors while letting genuine customers through. They can also help protect customer account information and passwords held online to protect your customers from identity theft. Companies like Forter even offer chargeback protection, meaning they are so confident of their detection capability that they are willing to absorb fraudulent transactions that might slip through their guards. Of course, you will be paying them for the extra service, but you should do a cost/benefit analysis to determine whether or not it's worth the investment for you to have that peace of mind.

If you own a brick-and-mortar type of business, here are some tips for you to reduce frauds and scams:

- Install an alarm system that has the capability of notifying you remotely when it is triggered. If you have expensive items in store, consider installing glass break sensors; these allow alarms to activate even before the crooks enter your store. Thieves are more deterred by the noise of an alarm than by the presence of security cameras because they can hide their faces with caps, masks, hoodies, etc. Your alarm system is your first line of deterrence.

- Install a CCTV system that covers the main entrance, shop floor and all your tills. Coverage at tills will help deter internal staff theft, capture transactions and even scammers who do quick change scams (whereby an individual targets inexperienced cashiers by paying for small-priced items with a large bill. Before the cashier can give back the correct change, the perpetrator confuses the cashier by asking for a series of money exchanges.)

- Place signs near your entrance, back door, and in the store informing would-be thieves that you have alarms and CCTV monitoring.If you use a cash collection service, ensure that you always give your cash to the same collector. If in doubt that a new personnel may not be from the legitimate company, don't hand your cash over.
- Train all your staff to recognize fake notes.
- Refund frauds are very common. Some scammers steal your goods, then print fake receipts of their own or steal receipts from your trash, then ask the store for a refund. My church member in the security industry assisted in the capture of a pair of fraudsters who stole thousands of dollars from different stores by refund fraud. One store's external CCTV finally captured one of the crook's car license plate and the police arrested them.

JOB & REWARDS SCAMS

If you get emails offering you a reward or a job with high pay and little effort, it's probably a scam. There are also fake online job interviews that are designed to steal your personal data so the scammers can use your information to hack into your accounts.

CRYPTO SCAMS

Given that many crypto exchanges have closed down and run off with their clients' money (including Canada's largest exchange Quadriga in 2019 and Turkey's largest exchange Thodex in 2021), how can you trust any crypto exchange? In an unregulated market, it is difficult, but here are some tips. A reputable crypto exchange should reveal the names of their management, the location of their office, and their contact number or email.

However, even large exchanges often don't list their phone numbers. It may simply be impractical for them to handle the volume of phone calls from users who don't understand how crypto works and who will waste their time asking educational questions. Instead, most crypto exchanges and wallet companies advertise their social media accounts on platforms like Twitter and Telegram.

The problem is that these legitimate companies cannot handle customer support via Twitter and Telegram, and this is where scammers jump in. As soon as you post your customer-related question on Telegram, a scammer using the same logo as the company private messages you to offer help. "How can I help you?" After a few exchanges, the scammer will offer to solve your problem if you will send them one Ethereum coin which they guarantee will be refunded once the "technical issue" is fixed. You should be aware that:

1. No legitimate customer support will initiate a

private message with you on a public social network like Telegram (they may do so after you login to your private trading account), and

2. no technical issue, like a delay in withdrawal, requires a payment of one Ethereum to be sent first to customer service, then refunded later in order for your issue to be fixed. The only time a fraction of a coin is needed is to pay the "gas" fees of an exchange or withdrawal. Such funds must already be in your account, not sent to fake customer service on Telegram. If you're trading on Binance, you need to have some Binance coin (BNB) to pay for the "gas fees" which pays the miners for their "proof of stake" or "proof of work," the consensus mechanism to confirm a transaction has taken place on the Blockchain. On nearly all exchanges, some Ethereum is needed is to pay for "gas fees" when you are swapping or withdrawing coins that exist on the Ethereum network (such as ETH, BAT, BNT, CVC, and OMG).

Never ever give your "seed" (a set of 12 or 24 words) that unlock your private crypto wallet. Your seed phrase is the English version of your 64-character private key that grants access to your funds on the Blockchain. No one but you should have your seed phrase or your private key. No legitimate customer service will ask you for your seed.

CHURCH & MINISTRY SCAMS

Last but not least are the scams that target Christian churches and ministries. Such scammers try to rip off pastors and donors. Some of them are low-tech, like scammers who bring children to church service to crawl around the sanctuary and steal from wallets and purses of unsuspecting church members while they're closing their eyes in worship. (This is why we have ushers and you should cooperate with them—they are looking out for you!)

There are more high-tech scams targeting Christians. Usually they involve impersonators learning some "Christian language" and offering personal words of prophecy to Christians. I've seen many fake "Steve Cioccolanti" accounts pop up on Facebook and YouTube. They set up a fake Facebook or YouTube account using my photo and pretend to be me. Then they start "friending" my friends and followers online. Then they start private messaging or emailing them, soliciting for funds. Here's the exact message of one persistent scammer who spams both Perry Stone and my social media accounts:

"Beloved, I don't know you in person but God knows you. God showed to me a revelation when I was on your profile to see things around you,I saw blessings but spiritual attacks holding on to them,in prayers,i saw a woman in the realm of the spirit monitoring and plotting delay in your life, with an evil mirror, and a motive to destroy. But as I speak to you now her time is up, Render hand of favour with Anything you can afford to these motherless foundation (CHARITY ORPHANAGE HOME FOUNDATION) in Edo State Nigeria, before 2DAYS with faith, as I Rise my hands towards heaven and pray for you they shall serve as point of contact where ever you are, you will receive double portion of grace to excel and total restoration of breakthrough in your life and in the life of your family. Contact or WhatsApp the MD in charge of the orphanage to get their details +234... [I blocked their phone number so you don't call them, but +234 tells you they're a Nigerian scammer] tell him I sent you. For it is not by might nor by power but of the spirit saith the lord (zechariah 4:6). You shall testify to the Glory of God in your life. God bless you..." Steve Cioccianti

A born-again Christian has the Holy Spirit inside his or her heart. Therefore, if you're born again, alarms should be going off in your spirit as soon as you read this. You should also be discerning enough to know this is a fake account. You can tell by several indicators: he misspelled my name, uses improper English, and has bad grammar. If you clicked on his profile (you should), you will see he started his account recently and has 0 followers, whereas my social media accounts have existed for many years and my genuine YouTube account has more than 300,000 subscribers. I do not private message strangers to give them personal words or ask them for money. I do not run an orphanage in Africa. My ministry is focused on preaching the Gospel, spreading God's Word to the world and making disciples of Christ. Whenever you wish to tithe or give online, always use a ministry's official website. Discover Church has two official websites: http://www.discover.org.au/partner and https://discoverchurch.online/.

"Happy Home Orphanage" doesn't exist. Scammers pull on Christian heartstrings by telling our partners the amazing work they are doing in Nigeria and the contribution will give orphans "a chance of a better future." What kind of Christian falls for these scams?

Surprisingly, we have found that Christians who don't like our channel, or sound most critical of our ministry, are the first to fall prey to such scammers. One YouTube subscriber complained publicly about how a video posted for free ended abruptly. She also complained that we spoke about money. But after she got what she thought was a personal word for her, she called the scammer's WhatsApp number to pledge money to the non-existent orphanage. From the perspective of a content creator, it's interesting to learn that scammers don't target only your fans, they also target your critics.

I personally reached out to this Christian critic to stop her from losing her money and she did not even thank me. It goes to show the poor judgment and lack of discernment of my critics. They liked the scammer's comment more than mine!

Our ministry spends on average 40 minutes to an hour each week deleting these scammer messages off our social media sites. This is why we prefer to interact inside our own online church app, which I recommend you join at: https://discoverchurch.online/

Does our ministry care for impoverished people and orphans? Of course, we do. Discover Church supports missionaries and their work in poor nations, but we vet them first. Before we give to a third party, you can be assured that we have personally met the ministry and seen their work on the ground, or else we have sent someone to verify their work is genuine and Gospel-centered. We will only support the kind of orphanage where God's Word can be shared and Jesus' Name spoken. Whenever you give to Discover Church, you are supporting the work of Christian ministry and you are automatically supporting missions work in foreign nations.

Never transfer your hard-earned money to someone whose work you haven't seen personally. Never donate to someone emailing you with a minister's name from a "hotmail" or "gmail" address. All legitimate ministries have their own domain names. Discover Church will always direct you to our official websites for your own security and peace of mind whenever you wish to make a donation. When in doubt, email us at info@discover.org.au and one of our partner care staff will assist you.

OTHER GENERAL TIPS

There are many other types of scams which we cannot go into detail in this book, such as dating scams, penalty scams, prize scams, telecommunication scams, etc. Below are some quick guidelines to help you protect yourself:

- Don't open attachments from strangers as these may lead to harmful malware being installed on your computer unbeknownst to you. When an email claims to come from my bank or credit card, I would first click on the "From" field to reveal the full email address of sender. If it ends in ".ru" it's a scammer from Russia. If it ends with "hotmail.com" you can be certain it's not from your bank.

- Don't click any link in emails or text messaging service that leads you to enter your username or password, especially to login to your bank account. Don't do it! They can easily steal your info and your money. Remember that giving away your personal login details is equally bad as giving away your money to scammers. Always login to your financial account via the provider's official website.

- As a rule, don't use the same password for more than one account or profile. This way if one account is hacked, not all your accounts will be compromised. Hackers succeed more often than you may think. Facebook, for instance, has had 6 known data breaches. The worst one in 2019 affected 540 million users—that's half a billion people! The latest hack in April 2021 resulted in the personal data of 533 million users being leaked online. The problem only gets worse for those users who used the same password on their other accounts.

- Never let someone claiming to be from a telecommunication company take over your computer (remote access). If you initiated the call to your service provider, that is different. They may ask you to grant them temporary remote access to see the problem you're describing. Apple, for instance, does this. But the scammers initiate the call to you. When you give them control over your computer, they can use it to hack your system without your knowing and then access your bank accounts, etc.

- Don't feel pressured to act by a caller or email, especially when they start threatening you. Some scammers claim you owe them money from past fines or overdue taxes, and unless you pay, they will arrest or deport you. Take time to think things through and seek professional advice. At the very least ask trusted friends who are in the IT industry whether they think it's a genuine email. You can make big mistakes acting under duress.

- When you fall victim to a scam, always make a police report and ensure you receive a copy of the report. This will ensure you have "proof" that you were a victim of fraud down the road. You may need the police report to prove that you were a victim of identity theft or claim insurance or a refund.

- Check your government's scam prevention website to see if an email or call you received is already a known scam. In Australia, scamwatch. gov.au is a great resource for seeing reports of the latest scams.

Chapter Five

THE GREATEST SCAM

THE GREATEST SCAM ON EARTH IS BEING PERPETRATED BY the devil. Jesus called him the father of lies. I call him the father of scams. There is no greater scam than taking millions of people to Hell while getting those people to believe they're going to Heaven. People believe the lie that they can ignore their sins, do a few good deeds in front of others, and end up striking it rich in eternity. It doesn't work that way. People have been conned by many forms of spirituality that claim you can meditate your way to freedom or climb your way into Heaven. If you get baptized in this church or take these sacraments or give to this charity, you'll be granted entry into God's Kingdom. That's not what God's Word says.

First of all, if that were true, then God the Father would not have needed to send God the Son to be born in the flesh. Second, Jesus would have died in vain. If you can save yourself and erase your own sins, then why did Jesus die on the Cross for our sins? Why did Jesus promise eternal life to the criminal who said, "Lord, remember me when You come into Your kingdom" (Luke 23:42) and promise damnation to the most religious people of His day (Matthew 21:31, Mark 12:9-12)? Third, Christianity would be a vain religion, because it states categorically that there is no other way to be saved but by repenting and believing in the sinless Savior, Jesus Christ. Fourth, all the preachers of Christianity from Peter and Paul to Billy Graham would all be liars, because they preached that sinners must repent, turn from their sins or face the fires of hell. Why would the best people on Earth lie?

In this world, it is easy to be misled. Don't be scammed or conned into thinking that if you do religious deeds, you can save yourself. No, your sins deserve to be punished and either you will pay for them yourself or you can accept Jesus' sacrifice on your behalf. He is the only Person ever to be born sinless of the Virgin Mary, to live without sinning, and to die for other people's sins. No one else is like Jesus.

The only way to be saved that is not a scam is through Jesus Christ, the Son of God. **His way of salvation is scam proof.** Don't be scammed by the greatest lie of all time, that there is another way to Heaven. Jesus did not say He was one of many paths. He said He is the Way, the Truth, and the Life (John 14:6). You must decide whether you believe Jesus is lying or telling the truth.

We should not come to Jesus with religious deeds to pay Him. Rather, we come to Jesus as people who have been scammed by the biggest con-artist, Satan, and who consequently feel helpless to get ourselves out of our predicament. It is this attitude of surrender that allows Jesus to step in and rescue us from a devastating loss.

To surrender to Jesus today, pray this pray out loud with your own voice:

~

"*Dear Heavenly Father, I've lost so much in my life—some of it is my own fault, some of it is other people's doing. I ask You to forgive me and give me a born-again heart to forgive others. I surrender my life to Jesus Christ, who is able to restore all I've lost and give me much more than I've ever hoped for—forgiveness of my sins, eternal life, and a place in God's Family. Thank You for dying on the Cross for me. Thank You for rising from the dead after 3 days of suffering for my sins. I call You my Lord and Savior. From this day forward, please use my life for Your glory, in Jesus' name I pray. Amen.*"

~

*I*f you've just prayed this prayer for the first time, congratulations! Tell someone about your decision. You can tell me at info@discover.org.au, subject: New Believer. I'd love to hear your story and help you get started on your new journey with God. Download a Bible on your mobile device and begin reading it daily. It is God's Love Letter to you and will give you wisdom and encouragement.

Also you need a spiritual family where you belong. Ask the Lord to lead you to a good church that teaches God's Word and not man's opinions or theological arguments. Those things sideline the importance of finding out your purpose in life. God has a good plan for you that involves a church where you form relationships with Christian peers and mentors! If you can't find one near you, I invite you to join online church: https://discoverchurch.online/

Chapter Six

JUSTICE PRAYERS

USE THESE SCRIPTURES WHEN YOU PRAY FOR restoration from an injustice, a theft or a scam. Speak them out loud—loud enough that you can hear it, the devil can hear it, and the angels of God can hear it. They are not reading your mind. They can't hear your thoughts! Remember the angel Gabriel told the prophet Daniel, *"Fear not, Daniel, for from the first day that you set your heart to understand and humbled yourself before your God, **your words** have been heard, and I have come **because of your words**,"* (Daniel 10:12 ESV, bold mine).

Angels do not come because of your thoughts. God doesn't answer unvoiced wishes. We should be happy He doesn't because we think a lot of thoughts we wouldn't wish to come true. Thoughts should be filtered by our faith in God's Word, then we should give voice to only what we truly believe. When we pray, we can be sure our thoughts align with God's will when we quote God's Word back to

Him. It's okay to personalize Bible verses and apply them to your life. God delights to hear you quote His own Word back to Him.

*H*ere are 22 of the best passages of Scripture I use to pray for justice and restoration after a loss. I also show you a model of how I would pray. Feel free to copy the model as is or adapt the wording as you feel led by the Holy Spirit. God watches over His Word to perform it (Jeremiah 1:12 ESV).

GENESIS 31:6-7
6 And you know that with all my might I have served your father.
7 Yet your father has deceived me and changed my wages ten times, but God did not allow him to hurt me.

Pray: Father God, thank You that You do not allow cheaters and deceivers to hurt me. Even if they cheat me ten times, I will come out stronger and better than before, just like Jacob did.

GENESIS 31:41-42
41 Thus I have been in your house twenty years; I served you fourteen years for your two daughters, and six years for your flock, and you have changed my wages ten times.

42 Unless the God of my father, the God of
Abraham and the Fear of Isaac, had
been with me, surely now you would
have sent me away empty-handed.
God has seen my affliction and the
labor of my hands, and rebuked you
last night."

Pray: Father, You rebuked Laban for changing Jacob's wages ten times. How much more will You rebuke my enemies who have cheated and stolen from me. The God of Abraham, Isaac and Jacob is with me and will not send me on His assignment empty-handed. I love to serve You more than dishonest men.

EXODUS 14:14
"The LORD will fight for you, and you
shall hold your peace."

Pray: Lord, forgive me for talking too much and defending myself too often. You are fighting for me, so I will hold my peace, stand still, and see the salvation of the Lord (2 Chronicles 20:17).

EXODUS 23:22
"But if you indeed obey His voice and do
all that I speak, then I will be an
enemy to your enemies and an
adversary to your adversaries.

Pray: Father, I commit to obeying You. Thank You for promising to be an enemy to my enemies and an adversary to my adversaries.

> ### LEVITICUS 19:11, 13 (ESV)
> 11 *"You shall not steal; you shall not deal*
> *falsely; you shall not lie to one*
> *another.*
> 13 *"You shall not oppress your neighbor or*
> *rob him. The wages of a hired worker*
> *shall not remain with you all night*
> *until the morning.*

Pray: It's wrong to steal, deal falsely and lie to another person. If I have ever done any of these things, I repent for my sins and ask You to wash me clean by the sinless Blood of Jesus Christ. I will not keep what is owing to another person overnight. I will not oppress or rob those who are close to me. I will restore everything I have stolen, therefore I can expect God to restore what's been stolen from me, in Jesus' Name.

> ### DEUTERONOMY 27:19
> 19 *'Cursed is the one who perverts the*
> *justice due the stranger, the fatherless,*
> *and widow.' "And all the people shall*
> *say, 'Amen!'*

Pray: Dear Lord, please curse the people who love

injustice. May the people who follow the Lord and all the people who seek justice say, "Amen!"

> ### DEUTERONOMY 32:4 (ESV)
> *4 "The Rock, his work is perfect, for ALL*
> *his ways are JUSTICE. A God of*
> *faithfulness and without iniquity,*
> *just and upright is he.*

Pray: Jesus is my Rock. I worship the Rock for His work is perfect, for all His ways are Justice. You are a God of faithfulness and without sin. Just and upright are You, O my Lord.

> ### PSALM 35:24-28 (NET)
> *24 Vindicate me by your justice, O Lord*
> *my God. Do not let them gloat*
> *over me.*
> *25 Do not let them say to themselves,*
> *"Aha! We have what we wanted!" Do*
> *not let them say, "We have devoured*
> *him."*
> *26 May those who rejoice in my troubles*
> *be totally embarrassed and ashamed.*
> *May those who arrogantly taunt me be*
> *covered with shame and humiliation.*
> *27 May those who desire my vindication*
> *shout for joy and rejoice. May they*
> *continually say, "May the Lord be*

praised, for he wants his servant to be
secure."
28 Then I will tell others about your
justice, and praise you all day long.

Pray: Dear Heavenly Father, vindicate me by Your justice, because I trust in Your justice. Do not let the thieves gloat or get away with it. May those who arrogantly taunt me be covered with shame. I will praise the Lord and I will tell others about Your justice, in Jesus' Name. Amen.

PSALM 37:22, 34
22 For those blessed by Him shall inherit
the earth, But those cursed by Him
shall be cut off.
34 Wait on the LORD, And keep His way,
And He shall exalt you to inherit the
land; When the wicked are cut off, you
shall see it.

Pray: I am blessed by the Lord, therefore I shall inherit land. I wait on the Lord, and keep His way, and He shall exalt me to inherit land. Though others try to steal my inheritance, the Lord will cut them off, and I will see it. My inheritance is secure in the Lord Jesus Christ.

PSALM 37:25-26
25 I have been young, and now am old; Yet
I have not seen the righteous forsaken,
Nor his descendants begging bread.

26 He is ever merciful, and lends; And his
descendants are blessed.

Pray: Father, thank You that the righteous are never forsaken and my children will never be in need. I am ever merciful. I lend. I have enough resources to help others and my children are blessed. They will always have abundance and provision. Make them wise to avoid deceivers and scammers. Deliver us from evil and evil people (Matthew 6:13). Help us to form the right relationships with people You are using to do Your mighty work on the earth, in Jesus' name.

PSALM 86:17 (NET)
17 Show me evidence of your favor. Then
those who hate me will see it and be
ashamed, for you, O Lord, will help
me and comfort me.

Pray: Heavenly Father, show me evidence of Your favor. Make me triumph over the plots and plans of my enemies. I know You have helped me and comforted me, and I'm so grateful for Your love.

PSALM 105:14-15 (ESV)
14 he allowed no one to oppress them; he
rebuked kings on their account,
15 saying, "Touch not my anointed ones,
do my prophets no harm!"

Pray: You allow no one to oppress me; You rebuke kings and powerful people for my sake. The Lord said, Touch not my anointed, do my prophets no harm! Satan, you have no right to touch me because I am God's anointed. Take your hands off me! Take your hands off my finances now, in Jesus' Name!

> **PROVERBS 10:2-3 (God's Word)**
> **2 Treasures gained dishonestly profit no one, but righteousness rescues from death.**
> **3 The LORD will not allow a righteous person to starve, but he intentionally ignores the desires of a wicked person.**

Pray: Righteousness is better than wealth. The Lord will not allow a righteous person to starve, but He will punish the dishonest and intentionally ignore the desires of the wicked. Lord, I pray, may You ignore the prayers of scammers!

> **PROVERBS 13:22**
> **22 A good man leaves an inheritance to his children's children, But the wealth of the sinner is stored up for the righteous.**

Pray: Father, it's Your will that I leave enough inheritance not only for my children, but also for my grandchildren. I believe the wealth of the sinner is stored up for the righteous. I am one of Your righteous, therefore I believe I receive the great, end-time transfer for wealth to establish Your covenant and build Your church. Thank You for opening my eyes to innovations and opportunities that come from You. In Jesus' name, I pray.

PROVERBS 20:17 (ESV)

17 Bread gained by deceit is sweet to a man, but afterward his mouth will be full of gravel.

Pray: O Lord, fill the mouth of every scammer with gravel. Let them not use their tongue to lie any more—to deceive or defame me anymore. Let them have difficulty talking until they repent and restore what they took, in Jesus' Name.

ISAIAH 54:14-15 (NET)

14 You will be reestablished when I vindicate you. You will not experience oppression; indeed, you will not be afraid. You will not be terrified, for nothing frightening will come near you.
15 If anyone dares to challenge you, it will not be my doing! Whoever tries to challenge you will be defeated.

Pray: Thank God whoever tries to challenge me will be defeated! I will not be terrified, I will not be afraid, and I will not experience prolonged oppression. Because You, O Lord, promised that I will be reestablished after a loss. You vindicate me in broad daylight (Psalm 37:6). I believe I receive it in Jesus' Name!

> ### ISAIAH 54:17
> *17 No weapon formed against you shall prosper, And every tongue which rises against you in judgment You shall condemn. This is the heritage of the servants of the LORD, And their righteousness is from Me," Says the LORD.*

Pray: I declare that no weapon formed against me shall prosper, and every tongue that lies about me will be condemned. This is the heritage of the servants of the Lord, and I am one of them! I am a servant of God! My righteousness does not depend on me, but on Jesus. My right-standing before God the Father has been conferred on me by the Lord Jesus. Thank You, Jesus!

> ### MICAH 2:1-3 (NIV)
> *1 Woe to those who plan iniquity, to those who plot evil on their beds! At morning's light they carry it out because it is in their power to do it.*
> *2 They covet fields and seize them, and houses, and take them. They defraud*

people of their homes, they rob them of
their inheritance.
3 Therefore, the LORD says: "I am
planning disaster against this people,
from which you cannot save
yourselves. You will no longer walk
proudly, for it will be a time of
calamity.

Pray: Father, I don't rejoice that my enemies will meet with disaster. I pray they repent and restore what they've stolen quickly, but if they don't, I am relieved that I do not have to take matters into my own hands. I refuse to stress or worry because of an injustice. I believe You are planning disaster against such people—such a disaster that they cannot save themselves from it. They will no longer be proud or act proudly. You said, "Beloved, do not avenge yourselves, but rather give place to wrath; for it is written, 'Vengeance is Mine, I will repay,' says the Lord" (Romans 12:19).

LUKE 18:1-8

1 Then He spoke a parable to them, that
men always ought to pray and not lose
heart,
2 saying: "There was in a certain city a
judge who did not fear God nor
regard man.
3 Now there was a widow in that city; and

she came to him, saying, 'Get justice
for me from my adversary.'
4 And he would not for a while; but
afterward he said within himself,
'Though I do not fear God nor
regard man,
5 yet because this widow troubles me I
will avenge her, lest by her continual
coming she weary me.' "
6 Then the Lord said, "Hear what the
unjust judge said.
7 And shall God not avenge His own elect
who cry out day and night to Him,
though He bears long with them?
8 I tell you that He will avenge them
speedily. Nevertheless, when the Son
of Man comes, will He really find faith
on the earth?"

Pray: Father, Your Son taught me to pray for justice like the widow who came to a judge to sue for justice. Therefore I ask by faith: Avenge me! Avenge me of my adversary! Avenge me of mistreatments and thefts, in Jesus' Mighty Name. I believe You hear Your own elect and You avenge us speedily. When You return, Lord Jesus, You will find faith for justice on the earth, because I believe You are the righteous Judge who will always do right. Praise Your holy Name!

ACTS 5:8-11

8 And Peter answered her, "Tell me
whether you sold the land for so
much?" She said, "Yes, for so much."
9 Then Peter said to her, "How is it that
you have agreed together to test the
Spirit of the Lord? Look, the feet of
those who have buried your husband
are at the door, and they will carry
you out."
10 Then immediately she fell down at his
feet and breathed her last. And the
young men came in and found her
dead, and carrying her out, buried
her by her husband.
11 So great fear came upon all the church
and upon all who heard these things.

Pray: Lord, You warned me about scammers who can even lie to the Holy Spirit and twist the truth inside the House of God. Ananias and Sapphira lowballed the price of something they sold and they were judged. I ask You to judge those who have lied to me about the prices of goods and services, kept back the fullness of an inheritance, and covered up a right or benefit that is due me, in Jesus' Name.

1 CORINTHIANS 6:9-10 (GNT)
9 Surely you know that the wicked will
not possess God's Kingdom. Do not

fool yourselves; people who are
immoral or who worship idols or are
adulterers or homosexual perverts
10 or who steal or are greedy or are
drunkards or who slander others or
are thieves—none of these will possess
God's Kingdom.

Pray: It is a fearful thing to lose your eternal soul and be separated from God for all eternity. Slanderers and thieves are listed among those who will not inherit the Kingdom of God. Those who slander or steal from me have bigger problems than me. I pray You will strike the fear of God into them to change their ways before it is too late. Do a miracle and cause them to repent and restore publicly what they did secretly. Therefore I do not fear them. "For there is nothing covered that will not be revealed, and hidden that will not be known," (Matthew 10:26).

GALATIANS 6:7 (NIV)
7 Do not be deceived: God cannot be
mocked. A man reaps what he sows.

Pray: Dear Father, I will not worry about scammers because no one gets away with sin. Whatever they sow will come back to them in multiple fold. I will keep sowing peace and walking in love. I will not grow weary in well-doing. I will not stop believing Jesus. I will not quit serving His church which is His Body. Whatever I do unto others is the same as doing it unto You (Matthew 25:31-46). I sow good seeds and my harvest is coming!

> **2 TIMOTHY 3:1-2, 8-9**
> **1 But know this, that in the last days
>   perilous times will come:**
> **2 For men will be lovers of themselves,
>   lovers of money...**
> **8 Now as Jannes and Jambres resisted
>   Moses, so do these also resist the
>   truth: men of corrupt minds,
>   disapproved concerning the faith;**
> **9 but they will progress no further, for
>   their folly will be manifest to all, as
>   theirs also was.**

Pray: It is the end times—a time when God's Word predicted people will love themselves more than others and love money more than integrity. These are men and women of corrupt minds. Yet I believe they will progress no further, and their folly will become obvious to all. I will keep following God's Word and my life will outshine and outlast the wicked whose lives will fade away, in Jesus' Name.

> **JAMES 5:4 (ESV)**
> **4 Behold, the wages of the laborers who
>   mowed your fields, which you kept
>   back by fraud, are crying out against
>   you, and the cries of the harvesters**

have reached the ears of the Lord of hosts [Lord of Sabaoth in the King James Version].

Pray: O Lord of Hosts, let the cries of those who have been defrauded and defamed come to You in these last days. You are the Lord of Sabaoth or the Lord of Hosts. This is Your title which best described You in the last days: the Lord of Heaven's Armies, the God of Judgment. Come and judge those who have withheld my dues and stolen my property, that I may serve You unhindered. Praise be to Your holy, awesome, and terrifying Name: the Lord of Sabaoth!

NOTES

INTRODUCTION

1. https://www.cnbc.com/2018/12/10/the-stories-of-madoffs-victims-vary-widely-a-look-10-years-out.html
2. https://www.theguardian.com/business/2009/jun/29/bernard-madoff-sentence

2. SEVEN-FOLD RETURN

1. https://www.richdad.com/school-of-hard-knocks

3. BIBLICAL JUSTICE

1. Stream teaching on prayer here https://vimeo.com/ondemand/guaranteedprayer or purchase CDs or DVDs on prayer here https://discover.org.au/bookshop/index.php?route=product/search&keyword=prayer
2. https://curiousmatic.com/colossal-failed-government-projects/
3. https://www.weaselzippers.us/127128-list-the-36-obama-funded-green-energy-failures/
4. http://museumofbadart.org/about-moba/
5. https://www.newstribune.com/news/opinion/story/2020/aug/22/your-opinion-money-wasted-for-bridge-to-nowhere/838494/

OTHER BOOKS BY STEVE CIOCCOLANTI

From Buddha to Jesus
(On comparative religion. Available in English, Cambodian, Chinese, French, Indonesian, Japanese & Thai)

30 Days to a New You
(Compact Plan for Personal Growth & Freedom)

30 Diás de Renovación Personal
(30 Days to a New You: Spanish Edition)

12 Keys to a Good Relationship with God
(Children's Book written with 6-year-old daughter Alexis)

The Divine Code: A Prophetic Encyclopedia of Numbers, Vol. 1 & 2 (Combined Special Edition)
(Discover the meaning of numbers)

Trump's Unfinished Business: 10 Prophecies to Save America (Paperback or Ebook)

Author's Central: http://amazon.com/
author/newyorktimesbestseller

Made in United States
Orlando, FL
20 June 2024

48108461R00059